(alive): Selected and new poems

(alive): Selected and new poems

Rhea Tregebov

Wolsak and Wynn . Toronto

Typeset in Garamond, printed in Canada by The Coach House Printing Company, Toronto, Ontario

Cover image: Bebe
Author's photograph: Luna Simić
Cover design: Coach House Printing Co.

Selections from *Remembering History* ©1982 Rhea Tregebov, Essential Poets series, Guernica Editions (Toronto). Selections from *No One We Know* ©1986 Rhea Tregebov, Aya (Mercury) Press (Toronto). Selections from *The Proving Grounds* ©1991 Rhea Tregebov, Signal Editions, Véhicule Press (Montreal). Selections from *Mapping the Chaos* ©1995 Rhea Tregebov, Signal Editions, Véhicule Press (Montreal). Selections from *The Strength of Materials* ©2001 Rhea Tregebov, Wolsak and Wynn Publishers (Toronto).

The author and publishers gratefully acknowledge the support of the Canada Council for the Arts and the Ontario Arts Council for their financial assistance.

ONTARIO ARTS COUNCIL
CONSEIL DES ARTS DE L'ONTARIO

The author thanks the Toronto Arts Council for its support.

The Canada Council | Le Conseil des Arts
for the Arts | du Canada

Many thanks to Roo Borson for her help in sorting through all the bad.
Y gracias a la vida, que me ha dado tanto...

Wolsak and Wynn Publishers Ltd
196 Spadina Avenue, Suite 303
Toronto, ON
Canada M5T 2C2

To my family

CONTENTS

From *Remembering History*

From *No One We Know*

From *The Proving Grounds*

From *Mapping the Chaos*

From *The Strength of Materials*

Move: New poems

From: *Remembering History*

1. *Life in the Primer*

We look   Sweet white milk
in a glass
yellow butter,
bread.

Our hands are folded
on the desk.
There is the dog
ball   kitten.
Things are as round
as their names.

Whether we turn back
or turn forwards,
the ball comes up
page after page
without changes.

There is Jane in pink,
in fuzzy sweaters.
She's always all ours –
never a hand, never
even a toe strays
off the edge of the page.
She suffers white ankle socks.

2. *On the Sidewalk*

Jane grows up   Birds die.
A boy twirls a cat
round by its tail.
Jane never would.

She bites into her O Henry,
snaps two red barrettes
into her hair,

and O arithmetic,
O geography,
O social studies!
she gets straight A's.

She's taken a vow
not to step on a crack:
she knows what could happen.

3. *Jane in the Streets*

Her poor mother's heart
must be broken. Jane won't wear
anything bright: black's
the rage.

It's not just the hands clenched,
the shouts, never a cheerful face.

What does she mean,
what does she mean,
saying, "I can't close my mouth
round an Arrowroot biscuit
anymore?"

When have we ever done her any harm?

4. *Life in the Diner*

We look again. Mother never said
learn what to hate.
Jane wipes blood onto her apron,
offers coffee.
Her education got her nowhere.

Six chickens for the knife: no time,
no time. In the kitchen she's
no martyr, she's the angel of death.
Each chicken claims its own;
her customers fatten, their mouths
open, close.

Jane turns away, busy
at the counter.
If it's a question of faith,
she believes in the diner
the way the cow believes
the sledgehammer.

The kids go home for lunch
like little packages –
all their corners tucked in.
Jane watches from the boss's kitchen.
They scream in the schoolyard
and it isn't fear: it's desire.

I think my grandmother's life was more simple.
I think she had problems that were more concrete.
Tend the children, tend the furnace
so we don't freeze, don't catch fire.
I think she let morning roll towards her,
got up and set the yeast rising.
She mended grey socks with black wool,
sewed a fine seam between cloth and nothing.
I think the war ended, she went out,
buttoned every button on her coat,
touched her hat, and it was a fine day.

What makes you sure
one thing is better than another?
I can walk down this sidewalk
with a bag full of groceries –
milk, butter, eggs, oranges, grapes –
I can walk all the way home
and never believe they were ever touched
by a single pair of human hands.
It's two days to Easter
and I can not buy lilies.
I can't quite place her death.
Walking back from the supermarket
I'm very careful of the eggs,
I was taught to be careful of the eggs,
never to break anything.
I'll break the skin of the grapes
against my tongue, but the eggs
I'll swallow whole.
What makes you sure?
I can live in one house my whole life
and never look out onto the yard
and see the bushes pressing their green paws
against the wind, avid, angry as I am.
Everything wants to live.
Me too.
Everything wants to live forever.

ECHO

1.

After so many forks scraping on plates the
men are talking about Le Corbusier. The
ribs of the rocking chair press into my back:
damn, I cough on pie, some scratching piece
of apple in my throat. "More tea?" The beat
of their conversation falters, they smile,
no.

2.

Nothing hurts. It's an oven outside and
the sun presses down on my back. I wipe
my lip and see sweat mix with the blood.
Drops fall from the cut onto the dirt, the
carrot seeds, into the furrow. I clear
my throat, call Jenny from jumprope to
help.

3.

Now with everything put away, every-
thing under control, I have time.
Examining my hands I find the scab
still puckering the skin; it was an
unexpected opening. Before he can
ask a question, before he can think
of reprisals, I tell him. I say,
love,

From: *No One We Know*

(ALIVE)

1. *Not happy*

The cars must be warm
with radios on.
I look after one corner at a time
and at lunch hour and after work
the street opens up, shows itself raw
like inside a mouth, letting them out
people going to work.
I don't mind looking.
The tidy boys talk all they like:
nice narrow scarves, narrow coats.
They make the world
and I get to live in it.
The streetlights come on
of their own free will,
not happy but alive.

2. *Bring it with you*

It might not have been me, it might
have been someone not to be refused
they answered when I rang the bell;
it was out of habit they said come in.
I wanted to put my coat on a chair
and one of them said excuse me but
that's mine I'm sorry but we can't have
you in the house. You bring it with you.

3. *For the edge*

Peel this egg and you have an egg
a face under the face
like yours with the eyes closed.
Tap, tap, it gives way
comes apart in bits.
Tap, it's how you find yourself
when it gives way
like the cane taps
for the edge.

4. *Too much world*

Cut yourself
and the world rushes in.
You could die
from too much world in you.

I was afraid of things
that turned me inside out,
of being crazy. I lived
inside a line that told me
where I was and what I wasn't.

But you can make love.
The world can enter
without wounding you;
it can come in.

5. *I could put*

I'm to understand you meant it,
out of the blue. What do you
mean? I meant I meant this
if there was a thing I could put
my hand on you see you know
it comes out in patches I meant
a hula hoop on a concrete step
out of the blue
I mean the threshold,
stepping off

6. *This is where*

It's in the nature of solids
that a hand pressed against the glass
flattens but doesn't fill the window.
This roaring. It stops being water
and comes out to fill the room.
Put tea in a cup
it fills the cup, put it in a saucer
it fills the saucer. It would
try to fill the floor.
This is where I stop being me.
I open my mouth and empty myself
everything comes out.

The sherbet glasses in this Chinese restaurant
are authentic, you know. Exactly like the ones
in the delicatessen, the facets blunt, cloudy,
durable. I have something. I have a real coleslaw
dish, thick white oval with a green stripe. My
grandfather, you don't know him, isn't thinking
of anything as he steps inside. Nothing to match
that cool and dim, the floor swept clean, familiar.
He smoothes his apron and rests a hand on the
meek surface of wood. All along the long counter
the customers turn, nod. The grey cat touches the
hem of his trouser with the white tip of her nose.
I was never there, the only place on earth I exist.

ON THE PHONE

The phone in your hand, everything in
the kitchen agrees, listen. The voice in
your hand is your mother. Her body is
gone, she took it away a long time ago
but she left you this voice, words in
Russian, Yiddish; you have no mother
tongue. Just a voice that means to hurt
you. The kids are at school, the kitchen
agrees, you're alone, you're grown up, you
were a good girl. You love your mother.
The voice doesn't think much of you, listen.
Here's a list of what you did what you do
what you'll do wrong. The voice refuses
to live in time, listen. Why is the phone
in your hand? Listen, you didn't teach
your hand what to do, you didn't say no;
you hung on to the good child. Hang up.

Dry summer, 1960. This sky promises
nothing, wide-open. Sundays I take my bike
all the way down Carruthers to McPhilips.
Carruthers goes inside-out just past the tracks;
the houses dos-à-dos, some turned towards me
some turned away and I know why:
farmhouses went where they wanted;
there weren't any streets then.
I ride on past the stucco garages, past
where they give in to the baseball field;
the scoreboard spells three-quarters
of my name. This is what I do,
it never occurs to me it's real life.
I'm imagining what I'll buy
at the K-Mart. I have my own money,
I can get whatever I want
but the key rings and doorplates
never have my name on them.
Between the aisles, my eyes sore
from the colour, I'm excited at the same time
I'm sad, what do I want

Six Chocolate Donuts

That girl walking down Warren Road
with six chocolate donuts in a bag
setting a foot on each square of pavement,
rattling at the bars —
she can walk on the sidewalk
but not the grass.
Just now she feels free.
She picks up a newspaper
from the park bench. It says
these are the options:
a life empty of everything
but pain; a life empty
of everything but work;
a life empty of everything
but money.
She puts the paper down.
Someone could decide
she has the wrong look on her face.
If you lose control, she thinks,
they take everything you have away.
She eats one of the donuts,
walks away, thinking,
they let you know anything
but your own strength.

From: *The Proving Grounds*

FAITH IN THE WEATHER
for my sister-in-law, Judy Tregebov
killed in a care crash January 1987

I have to travel through so much weather to get to you.
I'm travelling at 30,000 feet, at 600 miles an hour,
my suitcases full, flying into sadness.
Over Manitoba all I can see is
marks on the absolute snow, the weather,
the curlicues of the big, fancy river.
This gut pain, for you, for anyone else I can imagine dead at 38.
I think how we each stood by a window, a country between us,
examining the story of our hands, thinking
about next Wednesday, about the spring.
All our fine, our beautiful wandering certainty, our faith.
Your life run head on, run through too fast.
How long between now and your last Sunday.
You perhaps seeing it come towards you forever;
your heartbeat, like an athlete's, infinitely slowed
to catch that last sweet second forever,
to breathe it all in.

VITAL SIGNS
March 1987

1.

When we almost lost him, I almost lost myself –
the taste of being alive like water after it's been frozen.
On the train to Kingston, to an appointment
with what I couldn't imagine as my life,
thinking, *I am somewhere.* Then the train comes out of its blackness
and the conductor announces, formally,
like the doorman at a ball: "Belleville."
And I *am* somewhere; writing this, am somehow real.
Belleville, where words bring me back to myself.

2.

Everywhere across the world it is 3:00 a.m.
& doctors are standing in the bright, medical halls
telling parents their child will live
or will die or may live. We're lucky.
A day or two later we go to a Chinese restaurant
and observe, beside the bruised steel coat rack,
the ornate, indecipherable face of one of their gods.

3.

They say *respiratory arrest* as if a law has been broken,
which it has. His father there to see his last breath go
and come again, that small mouth under the doctor's mouth,
then under the kindly machines. I come and see them all by his bed
and *what* is the word I am left. *What   what.*
They pick me up I say *what.*

4.

Make My World a Safe Place.
We bring the pamphlet home with him from hospital.
Like everyone, we try; we pick up all the straight pins,
fasten safety catches, stroller him to peace marches.
But not the gods
                who make us the gift of this child,
give him my sickness, take his breath
and then give him back to us to live
with this sickness.

5.

In weeks of subjunctive I discover
love a fluid, love contained
by the kind of days, and the long nights it is given;
it can sicken, and heal, and sicken,
and strengthen in a gaze.

The cold wind holds the tulips' bloom
this cold, endless spring we survive
inside the beautiful, delicate little cage
of his breathing. Our sickness, our tiredness,
the little love left us he forces
like the stolen forsythia of March.

AT 3:00 OR 4:00 OR 5:00 A.M.
March–June 1987

the green plastic of the respirator mask, my face watching
the green plastic of the mask hold your small breath,
drawn and released, your sleeping face calm
through the crib bars, against the crib bars,
my face watching your small battle gear,
your plastic breath travel the clear hose to the air compressor,
your extra lung, my steel help, steel hope,
clear plastic hope when your choking, your sure death
jerks me to the realistic kitchen,
the ritual medication, the refrigerator's pure light,
watching for your choking, your sure death
as my automatic fingers prepare the glass vial,
the chilled bronchodilator I believe in.
I believe in modern science,
the glass vial, the dial of my watch
counting the ten to twelve minutes of your miracle,
my salvation, the ten to twelve minutes
I grip your sleeping face calm against the crib bars,
grip the names of your sleeping features –
cheeks, eyes, nose, mouth – features of my salvation,
drawn and released, the names of my mother, my father,
the gods, name of my solitary childhood self, the child
alone in the strict hospital room, without mother, father,
the gods, child alone with each *acute exacerbation,*
alone with the ritual hope, ritual fear, pure motherless light.

I can almost see the room – no, not see, breathe it.
I can almost breathe that airless room in the story.
A true story, which was told me, but which is mine.
The mother puts her hand on her daughter's forehead.
The daughter is gasping like a creature not made for this room.
Her chest hurts, the thin stretched muscles on her thin ribs hurt,
the wiry ones that tighten along her throat hurt,
even the nostrils gasp and gasp; poor fish.
Something has laid its hand on her chest and it presses and it presses.
There is no doctor for days, there is no medicine
or the medicine doesn't work or hasn't been invented
and it has been days and days with not enough breath to sleep
or the medicine gives her nightmares or hallucinations:
the blood sings in her brain and her mother must pull the sheets tight
tight across the mattress, tight as the corded muscles of her throat
but they are never smooth enough and mustn't let her sleep
because sleep may kill her, the airlessness may creep
into the last empty corner of her lungs and then where would she be?
Not in the room, which becomes smaller and smaller;
there are only the two of them, the rest of the world has closed its eyes.
There are only the two of them and the only help is her mother's hand
on her forehead and her mother's voice which at last says it,
says it's alright to die if she has to, her voice
which at long last allows her daughter the death she may need.
Her mother's hand on her forehead, permission in her own hand,
she closes her eyes and the room rocks itself,

the room is at last at ease. My mother never said that.
Where would I be if I was or I still am the girl in the story,
who did not die, whose mother said what cannot be said,
what I wish never to have to grant or have granted to my one son,
the right to die, to give up,
to close the eyes as I do mine on my girl
and my boy and my true story, where would I be?

Here – you take it. I'm tired.
I like this – you at the wheel, the car nosing into darkness,
blind country on each side of the highway; the odd road sign
flaring in the high beams; blues you taught me to love on the radio.
We're back home, back in family. We both think of the baby,
still unwell, resting fitfully as your parents absorb the TV's
blue information. You turn off the motor and the Northern Lights
are cool, cool, the sky crowded with emptiness.
They remind us warmth is an aberration in the universe.
No one explains them.
This is our last resort, cottages winking like stars.
Tonight you aren't too tired to talk. This dock, you say,
you think of as your sister's, Judy, dead at 38,
her husband at the wheel. Under the cool gaze
of a solo streetlight, we don't want to think that it, our life,
is not Paris, not baroque logic elucidating medieval happenstance,
but a narrow wooden path raised from the cold touch
of the shallow waters of a northern lake,
the handrail disappearing pointlessly on the right.

STONECROP: NOTES TOWARDS AN ELEGY
August 1988
for Brian Shein

1.

It's the very tip of August, Brian,
and I'm walking home with the grocery bags slung over my wrists,
thinking only about the remarkable difference
between the price of salmon fresh and salmon frozen,
between bagel day of and day after.

It's easy to forget you were a cook (the meals you cooked!
the trouble you took with us, took us through!)
because for so long you had no kitchen; or if a kitchen,
no chairs, or if chairs, no pots or pans.

I have these bags of groceries and am alive,
walking down the street past everyone's yard,
they all have gardens, yards and gardens – lobelia, black-eyed Susan,
periwinkle; stonecrop, carpet bugle, snow-in-summer in the rock
          gardens,
the scent of alyssum in ours today makes me almost crazy,
here at the end of summer, and you
dead since I don't remember which day in June.

2.

For the butcher's apprentice, the former farmhand,
men who give up a finger to work or fate,
the mind's eye, permanently surprised at what is missing,
completes the loss, again and again makes whole their hands.

I keep completing the loss of you, Brian, drawing you into life
with mind's eye, mind's heart, heart's mind – whatever will bring you
          back.
Does every thing here now remember you, because incomplete?

3.

The end of day, the end, even, of desire
we press into the pillow to become what we once were:
part of it all, sweet sweet sweet in the darkness.

4.

Your life goes on without you, to our astonishment.
Here in August you get mail from universities, agencies,
who want you for all that we wanted, still want for you;
all that you deserved: the awards, the good jobs, days.

Goes on in me, who wants you back; to show you the new house
I talked and talked about. To hear you tell me, delicately,
never to keep the lid on while the pasta's cooking.
To read your next article in the September issue, and the next.

5.

The brain cosy in its nest of bone
understands as true and impossible that we die.
The body has only one life and yet there is some sort of life
that looks out of a dying body, impassive.
How you looked stubbornly at us all
for the five weeks between when the stroke took your speech
and the cancer finished you off.
Your eyes flicking through the lines
as you read our faces, stubbornly managing
the necessary syllables for the nurses: "no" "hurts" "pain."
And when your lover kissed you: "thank you."
I thought these weeks would get me used to your dying,
get me the chance for a decent goodbye. What you bid me,
one afternoon, was the sight of your arm
free of the chaos of the sheets
like Michelangelo's slaves of the marble.
Your arm so white, still alive.

My hands with the earth of the garden still on them,
dirt worked under the nails, into the creases of knuckle, palm,
life line, heart line. Sullen smell of diesel exhaust.
Bathurst Street shudders as the trucks grind uphill.
The perennials, persistent, shiver under my hands,
garden sloping steeply down to root in concrete.
This garden not of my own making,
a hard and rocky place I came into,
poor soil where succulents thrive (sedum, portulaca),
my stone crop, stone garden.
Unmanageable thing, living, unbeautiful,
the insistent labour of two summers has not kept from flourishing.
This, the stony place given me.

I get to the corner the way I get from one day to the next:
abstracted, mostly afraid, not entirely located in my body.
I get from one day to the next mostly afraid
while the boy in the playground at Huron Street,
who must be seven or eight, slides the toe of his black, shiny,
rubber cowboy boot along the black, shiny slick water atop the ice;
observes its wake, the bent, cold-burnt blade of grass afloat in its wake,
and underneath it all, the earth, cold and thrilling beneath the cold
rubber sole of his boot, and in his boot his foot, in his foot
the warm blood running, him. It is false spring at the end of January,
plus eight degrees and the water is running, it is running enough
to make you believe spring. The boy can't remember how cold it was
yesterday, can't hold winter in his mind. And here I sit,
by the equipment issue at the Athletic Centre, writing this,
and, god almighty, don't know how I got here.

From: *Mapping the Chaos*

Saturday at dinner, as we spoon into dessert
(crème anglaise with raspberry sauce on one side
chocolate on the other), our friend, who is a physicist,
speaks to us of time as yet another human
fallacy. That it's only through the usual egotism
of our species that we imagine its existence;
that looked at properly it may well have no beginning
or end to it. I probably don't understand him fully,
despite my ignorant love for physics.
But I have experienced something like
the a-chronological, standing for brief seconds
not in time, absorbed in some moody
perception, shop window; caught in stasis, being –
how glad I am of the forsythia today, for instance,
how it keeps coming back and coming back –
if that's what he means.
And I have felt the elasticity of time,
especially its slowness in those moments when
I was moving at or above the earth's surface,
the news of someone's death the event
that splits time into *before* and *after*.
As though in those moments *in between*
my grief for someone else left me
perhaps immortal, not part of time. I link this
with the desire I feel sometimes for death;
the wanting it all to stop, to stop, to step
outside of it all, outside of
everything the mind frets over busily,
all the questions that are for me anything
but philosophical. The questions I call
suffering; the question, I guess, of time,
of trailing the long long freight train
of our lives: the accumulated memories of this

bit of light striking that plane, smell
of decayed oak-leaves a resonance in the primitive
brain. All these things packed in electrical
circuits in the walnut our bony skulls
protect, synapses flickering like
the prettiest Christmas lights so that
if surgeons stimulate *that* bunch of cells
we taste our mother's breast milk; *this* bunch
and it's pale red tulips by the concrete steps
at Matheson Avenue. That the transparency we
imagine of ghosts is the transparency of memory.
A collision of times. And who can tell me why
it is that often when we make love I am among the arches
under the New Sacristy in Florence where
we went up, eighteen and nineteen years old,
to see for the first time
Michelangelo's tomb for the Medicis? What
does lovemaking have to do with
Renaissance art? Or is it arches, is it
the caves down there, is it that
the trigger this moment is just death,
that I'm thinking of how, making love, we go
into it, the great current of procreation, time?

My grandfather, absolutely foreign,
his sheared sealskin angular hat set right
straight on the middle of the top of his head. Not
cowboys, but his buffalo coat I saw only
thrown over the hood of the car to keep
the engine warm and thought he was wrong again,
in his Old Country fashion, but he was right,
you *can* keep the inanimate warm with something
that was once alive. "My country." The stones
of Odessa, the Black Sea was a terrible thing,
black as oil and cold, I thought, steps went
straight down to it and the waves licked at them.
Terrible too the cold avenues of Winnipeg, where
the Jews slotted themselves into streets named
Selkirk and Salter. Tea with lemon,
sucked through a sugar cube, poppy-seed roll
in the oven. And outside, the smell of wet wool,
clean city smell, the taste of the screen door
and my own blood – how our flesh loves metal
at that temperature, cold that sings in the brain
like a fever. And it wasn't just winter,
it was the squeak, squeak of the swings
my father and his brothers made, the heart-
shaped, spade-shaped leaves of the lilac bush,
my father turning, turning, spading the black soil.
What does a Jew do with a garden? We grow beets
for the borscht, rhubarb, dill for the pickles,
cukes; we grow peas for the kids to pick and eat,
that never see the table. But when "Don Messer's
Jubilee" came on TV, we turned it off. The family
rose as one and turned our backs because there
is no irony in country music; you have only
the one hand, not the other.

It's pure and straight and true.
Unlike life on the outside, or life
on the inside. Unlike being both here
and there or neither here nor there.
Unlike the red, cold, sweet and
sour heart of beet soup.

DPs

I'm on the subway and I'm in Gail's backyard,
the prim outlines of her father's garage
stuffed full of bits of electrical things,
and the sun is bumping hard against stucco. We're squatting
at the edge of that white, the dirt smells like dirt,
and I see her six-year-old face, bangs cut straight
across, my best friend. She knows me. She can look
right through my head. Her mother is in the kitchen,
working bread dough the colour of her hands, stuffing
air into the dough. And it rises Vitebsk, Charadetz, Lublin.
She pushes it down, pulls it in. Rochel, Basya,
Chana, the red hair, the broad-boned cheeks,
the round glasses. She pushes it down, pulls it in.
Was it Gail's mother my mother, born lucky, born here,
gave her first lipstick? Raspberry Glow, Peach Melba.
You can't stop the past. The house stuffed with smells.
Eat it and live. Soon, soon but just for now
we're busy with dirt, busy with the high, square
green of the garden, beans moving
upwards on wire to the top of the sky, just now I'm
on the subway, in Gail's backyard.

ELEGY: ABRAHAM BLOCK, 1917 –1993

My father's brother *the first to go* of these three,
men who jostled one another like boys, wrestling
on the lawns. The first to go where?
This death a Winnipeg light, so steady
every edge is clear, every object, person,
stands separate for a moment from the flow of things;
solitary in flux, in the world. So I am there
on the lawn, where I feel the world split into gender.
Impossibly small and female watching these men
who never raised a hand tumble, push, release
the power they withhold for us. I watch them laughing,
their paws at each others' limbs, male and indestructible.
Men who crush men's hands when they shake them. On purpose.
Sunday afternoons from a doorway I watch Abe sleep
in his long johns on the frayed couch, his one
half day of rest, his sons circling. His blunt
gentle hands improbably stroking the cat,
smoothing my hair. "Feel this," he'd say
his voice tender with awe at our girl-ness,
his shaved cheek scented, delicate against ours.

Even the memory shames me and
it has happened more than once, my desperate
confusion nights when my son and I both have had far
too little sleep and morning finds me beside myself;
some wicked shouting thing, scared
and terrifying, stands beside my real,
good self and over him, a woman possessed
by the usual (fear). Thinking *he'll get sick* by which
I mean *this is not the life I want.*
I get my body confused with his.
I get my body confused with his
when I can't keep him safe, the way
I used to, when he was
my body. I get my body
confused with his, and it's
wrong and it hurts him,
I don't know how much.
          I imagine him, my son,
fifteen or twenty years from now,
a tolerant adult, forgiving me,
reading this and understanding,
like all the young, only
the extravagant, the outrageous claims
of motherhood, their oppressiveness and his own
imperative to escape them. Me.
Like all young men. No one will ever
be a part of his body.
          I think of the daughter I might have had,
will never have. So many holes in the universe.
Like the time at the farmhouse we looked up at the sky
and felt night fall off the mountain,

the hundreds of stars spilling out, lost
like the absences in our lonely bodies.
Or me shouting that morning in the beautiful hotel room
It costs too much!

IN THE NURSING HOME, 1966

Funny how the young are fascinated by
the old – their corporeality, the veins
fretting hands, the terrain all surfaces
become. My allotted three hours pass
on the given volunteer Tuesday or Thursday
in the telling of some story the old tell,
a story with characters and plot and
meaning – *this* happened in my life
and then *that* and *he* was the boy
I loved, we lived, if not happily
ever after, long after and that
was our life. Light rains into the room
from the leaves of the tall summery
elm in front; in sparse Winnipeg
this elm rises tall, as if
we are somewhere else. It means
the river is nearby. In this light I
thrill to the story, thrill mostly,
doubtless, to my own goodness. I am
patient and kind, good like my good
mother though even as I think this,
I think of my mother's own story, what
she is in the midst of paying
for her goodness, and the hard
voice in me says *not me*. The next
Tuesday or Thursday the story
will be the same and the same
and it will close round my throat;
then the voice will come up, saying
I'm not going back, Mom,
I can't stand it.

The story of what we've done
with our own lives we live with
but don't wish on our children:
my mother will smile, as if she is relieved,
as if she is glad to be thinking
I am not her enough to not be her.
But that first day the top of my head
is saturated with goodness as
I ride home on the orange and yellow
bus, the summer smell of its orange
plastic seats, more sun outside its windows.

CONFESSIONAL POETRY

The wrong I've done, I've done
at the kitchen sink: washing dishes
while my cousin and his wife – who
sang beautifully, she still sings
beautifully though she's not now
his wife; she was pregnant with their
first child and sick all the time;
they were visiting us at the American
college town we lived in and we too
were sick, homesick for family, and
they were good to us, are still, each,
individually good to us – my cousin
and his wife had gone to bed early,
and I stood over the supper dishes,
an elaborate supper that had only made
her sicker (escargot in garlic butter!),
I stood singing in my off-key, half-
assed voice, half in love, no,
completely in love with myself, till
my cousin called out, older, annoyed
and amused, "Why are you singing?"
pained, and I stopped. I think of it
still with shame, I'm good at shame
if not musical. I didn't know then
how well she sang, didn't know half
of how much I was in love with myself.
I was young, I didn't know how much
their separation would fracture my
notion of love, two such good people
bad for each other. I wonder
now where my husband was, wonder
that my singing never pained him,

more than half in love with me, I
suppose, to have put up with that.
But it wasn't just singing and self-
love, it was something worse: in that
same kitchen there was the Hungarian
graduate student whose pragmatic attitude
hardened me against her; she would
bring the most elaborate chocolate
tortes to dinner while we cooked,
that was the agreement, and I was,
again, washing something, the coffee
pot, we wanted some bitterness
to counter the rich dessert. "You've left
some suds on the pot," she pointed
out, and that's where I drew the line,
that was where the friendship ended.
I never had her back. How can I be
like that? It's some lesson I've learned
from some other woman, my mother,
my mother who never drew
the line between herself and her mother.
How hard I draw it. I can think
of other stories, just one or two,
all of them with water running over
my hands and light coming in
some window, but it isn't about
domestic peace, it's me, what I keep
doing wrong, how I can't forgive myself,
won't forgive others so I bash
against the walls of the world,
against other people –
this stubborn, foolish thing in me
I haven't yet let go.

Behind the rusted bent tin of garbage cans,
the dull grey sharp at the folded edges,
patches gone to foil, the red lace of decay,
through the thin cloth of the striped T-shirt
splinters in the skin of the back against brown
fraying wood in the smell of rot, in the smell
of darkness where the lilacs' salt-green leaves
dig air, or in the white atmosphere above the grass
between white stucco and white picket fence,
along the soft dusty dirt, the gentle dirt
of the garden where worms are, where things are alive,
the boy is hiding. He doesn't come though his mother
call and calls, he's too small to be lost this long.
Why is he hiding? His mother calls but he doesn't come
until he's found and when he's found she hits him
with the belt until the pain stops being pain,
until he's not there: he's hiding. He's not there.

Now

You're turned as always away from me on the bed.
I turn towards you in the dark. I can't leave you be,
my arm goes round you now when I turn
and press my face to your back, the skin of your back,
that same teenaged, sun-brown back you owned
the first sight I had of you, the feel,
that boy on the beach, the same boy, now, I shield,
perpetual boy my hand would save.
Nearly twenty years, now.
The "o" of my ring misshapen, the gold ground down.
I'm the girl who fingered her grandmother's thin band
in disbelief – that grandmother dead now fifteen years,
the gold worn off cell by cell,
through the pressure of my hands, my hands' work.

I want to stop being wonderful.
I want to put my head down on the desk
and not lift it up. I want to stop running
round and round the track. I want not to try.
I'm at the retreat, among writers and wildlife.
Elk stalk elegantly across the page.
They raise their heads and look at me,
asking, what's wrong with *you?*
I've had it with sentience.
I want to lie down in the cold November night
and look at the companionable stars,
and not get up.

The young woman curls in the yellow booth of the donut shop,
head forward, dark hair she tucks behind an ear as she worries
her pencil across the page. I can see the irregular blue & white
checkerboard, the little boundaries, computer-generated country
of shaded paths, whorls, lacunae, currents. She touches the pencil
to her mouth, then to her forehead. I remember that dread,
remember being young, being in offices, posed suddenly before
the cold machinery of the world and my place in it; the acrid
vapour of fear rising from the page, from the hopelessness
of trying to shepherd my reluctant, unfinished self into those
squares, those rectilinear rivers, when my life felt
undetermined; I might be anyone. How to brave out so many
unanswerable questions: *Where do you begin? Do you go on?*
Where do you end? I who might be anyone. But the young woman
looks to me determined, her pencil shapes its reply. I leave her,
head south down Bathurst Street in the hot September haze
to the school ground where I can see my son in his shorts
and dinosaur T-shirt. He is bunched with his friends
playing "Ledgers"; the group unspools and
my son's arm reaches back, he flings the ball fiercely
at the school's brick wall and fiercely it comes to him.
A tall boy with a baseball glove catches it, my son calls
out an order, the two change places, all *is* order,
I stand there watching and think, marvelling,
He fits in! This playground is his, this boy
knows all the rules, this son who is not my son,
not mine his ease across this surface of lines and
boundaries, I wonder, I do, at where
this child came from, where he will go.

THE DINNER TABLE, THE TULIP

So what do we do with this,
this world, this uncertain spring,
the tulips still holding, things green and cold.
Take the tulips, composed, driven to yellow or rose
from their chilly green, given to order,
unfolding. The colour they move towards
held for a day, or a week, contingent
on the weather, accident. Then paling or darkening
into other shades, then the quick
or slow decomposing. Coming to grief.
To being not tulips. Does rot
have its own order? I think not.
Theorists see things moving
to degeneration, some, and looking down,
I might be inclined to agree, skidding down
to an agreement since more than the weather
this spring is uncertain. Systems large
and small are flawed, disintegrating.
Think of anything: my respiratory system,
the world's. Today I run along the cul-de-sac
in the swanky end of our neighbourhood.
As always, there are vans parked in the driveways.
Things are being taken care of, expensive systems
in need of maintenance. The rest of us
are short on money, time, love.
And you so careless, the roof needing repair,
plaster crumbling from the living-room ceiling,
faith battered, struck by dilemma. Ah you.
It's a good thing it is spring, my faith still holding,
in me, this body running along concrete,
however the lungs rasp. Spring inclines me
elsewhere, to lean towards other theories –

anti-chaos, the universal yearning
towards order. Setting the table just so.
The tulips in the right vase.
Yearning, yes, the scientist on TV wanting
it to be the case that we are at home
in the universe, that life is inevitable,
"the consequence of broad avenues of possibility,
not back lanes of improbability." Although,
agnostic, I might settle for back lanes.
I've loved their rough edges, seamy sides:
rusted garbage cans overturned, the
opportunity for scrounging, the
possibility of unexpected plenty.
A clump of fat white violets beside the garage
and beside them, blue ones, their pansy faces
attentive. Not an aberration but a plan.
Agnostic, I bless those looking
for "a science of emergence, of complexity,"
looking for a way to model complicated systems
like the dinner table, the tulip. And I
agree. The ultimate question not only
of science, but ours *why is there*
something rather than nothing.

From: *The Strength of Materials*

Subway Elegy

Sometimes what I want
is for you to lay your body on mine
so that I know my own extent,
know where to stop. Me,
not me. Who do I love and
where do I stop loving?
Nothing in my body mourns
the death of a star in Ursa Major.
But the woman in Sarajevo
her boy's ten year old life
leaking through her hands
staining the cheap sweater
she could have bought up the street
at Zeller's, the boy's Adidas sneakers
unlaced by the blast –
to her my body replies,
mouth drawn inward, teeth
pulling at my bottom lip
and I go for my own boy's unscathed
head, pull his body back to me.
My sensible boy, who has seen
all kinds of TV death unmoved,
the boy who looks up at me,
his breath indrawn, hand to my shoulder,
when three die in the subway crash
at our local stop:
It could have been me.

ELEGY FOR THE LIGHT
Forty-third parallel, December

All this December as the light diminishes
we eat sweet small oranges from Spain,
their quick-zip peels spraying tart
on our fingers, small suns we eat.

I get on the bus in daylight, abstracted;
spend some minutes absorbing the faces
of fellow travellers, and when I look up,
look up to a darkness come so fast –
as though these faces had drunk the light.
And I'm afraid my face also has gone dark,
extinguished.

The streetlights are on,
and I want to remember that the light will come back,
that it's because of the angle of the earth's rotation,
because we're in the temperate zone
that we have seasons,
that things change and change and change.
But this year even change has been disorderly.
Today in December the air bewilderingly mild;
my star-of-Bethlehem poking dumb
green spikes out of winter dirt
below the honey-locust tree just in time
for Christmas or a killing frost.

Smell of orange on my fingers,
I step onto the rubber matting.
The door opens.
I don't believe in resurrection.
I have one life: what
if it fills with darkness?

Home from a long trip I find
the familiar rooms grown wider, and
me suddenly small, on the broad streets
of childhood. Small, like that, and
lonely. It's lonely here.
We think that down here,
on the planet, there's abundance; that
it's out there that warmth is an aberration –
the scientist sending out messages
looking for intelligent life, thinking
he may have located a likely solar system.
I don't know.
Take my friend from the former Yugoslavia
sitting inland, strong fingers splayed
on her knees, cold, remembering the sea.
Or my aunt, also inland, adrift, her memory
riffling like ripe wind through a wheat field –
she wakes, cold and afraid, to bury the husband
dead three years now. It's lonely here.
Take me. I have only my own body.
I nod to the neighbour,
leave messages for my best friend,
eat dinner with the radio on.
Don't tell me about lovers
on the shadowy grass, foreheads close,
whispering a world. The delicate
joints of equipment adjust, slo-mo,
bend like sunflowers to catch a reply.
Me, I'm looking too.

1.

Name the countries that border Rumania.
I don't know.

2.

Moon in the branches.
A few leaves huddle in clumps,
shivering like sparrows.
The ones that have fallen pile themselves
in the precise pattern the wind wants.
What do I know? It's easy to believe
in constancy, to believe the moon,
say, despite its changes, has
always been there. It hasn't.

3.

What you don't know can't hurt you
is a lie. I've always been afraid
of knowing, not knowing. Think
of my grandfather, father, uncles
at the Seder table, waiting for the bad
word, the syllable gone wrong,
to raise their chorus of correction,
keep us from damaging God.

4.

But to move from not knowing to knowing –
there's a dangerous space. Where do you go
in between the not and the knowing, what
becomes of you?

5.

The gloss, boss of that instrument, dusted,
polished for thirty years and not much used.
Twenty years past lessons, stiff,
my fingers pick out notes on my mother's piano,
and they come into melody. Downstairs,
in the orderly basement, opening the rounded,
studded lid of a trunk, I find books,
and from the books, Hebrew characters
and they come into sound on my lips, come into words.

6.

Name the countries that border Rumania. No.
I didn't want to know, wanted
to believe only what the body believed,
to feel the sidewalk sun-hot
through my thongs, on my skinny shoulders,
to lick a lime-green Popsicle, and be
in my body, the body happy
and me, in it, happy of it.

7.

What I didn't let myself know
hurt me. What does my body
remember? My mouth knowing yours,
your body in me.

LIST (ELEGY)

"...leve como el agua y la harina"
[...light as water, dust]

Thin milk poured
into the glass:
starved, starved, it says;
then it's gone. So
you write up a list:
milk & eggs. Think
milk & eggs. This
is what you have to do
and not think *sorrow,*
not think *but, but.*
Only. Milk & eggs.
This is what you have to do.

INTO THE WORLD (ELEGY)

"Nature has no outline, but Imagination has."
William Blake, Notebooks

1.

I'm sober, and everyone else is drunk.
I'm always sober. Upright
on my barstool, people around me spilling,
buddy, into each others' pockets, raucous
breath in beery faces
and I'm outlined in black crayon,
I have edges.

2.

I have edges, but they bend.
One day I'm walking up an ordinary street
and everywhere I look women are waistless,
led by our bellies. We're walking
up the ordinary streets and don't know
what we're getting ourselves into,
don't know that our lives will no longer
be our own, they'll be
everyone else's.

3.

It's work bringing my boy into the world.
He's distracted, head cocked,
tuned to some tangential thought,
askance to what he really should
be thinking about, a primary
idea: being born. *Push,* they say.
I can't not. We're both
taken, part of something else.
Then, pushed, that first yelp
of air, joy, or terror, breathing
all on his lonesome. And he's
one person. And so am I.

4.

Other women speak of the alien
moment their good bodies went awry.
But for me, it was the usual,
a body I'd never believed in
having its way.

5.

I didn't ask to be born.
He's bent out of shape, the boy,
angry that he's not grown up, that he's got
a mother. So skinny sideways, he's a stick
of chewing gum wrapped in foil, can flex.
And he wants to test himself, press
against the edges; does chin-ups, curls.
Pushes against the hard air, against
the world and what it will and won't let him have,
until he's changed, shaped a new boy.

6.

Some mornings I turn my face to the window,
its sun, or cloud, and then turn away:
I didn't ask to be born.
To be shoved out into this,
where I am one person. *Push.*
I want to be saved from life. To be
still, under the ground, live
with stones and the hungry
roots of trees.

7.

Those mornings, even babies make me sad:
the way they love the world, the way
they let it filter through them.
Because I'm afraid they'll be spoiled,
go brown at their edges, like fruit;
that their lives will sour, curdle.
But by noon, the boy bangs into the room,
hungry, to bend the emptiness and, *buddy,*
the lush green world insists, *ah friend,*
this is no way to feel; turn to the window,
the lovely world, take all it wants.

A Really Good Run (elegy)

I finish my run and think
I'm so strong now, nothing could kill me:
not the dwarf star imploding in Alpha Centauri, not
the Toronto Humane Society van swerving to avoid a racoon.
Not living beside Lake Ontario, not Devon cream or rare
roast beef, chlorinated, fluoridated water. Not booze,
drugs, sex, black ice on the sidewalk. Not seeing my aunt
go down my front steps, whispering, *It hurts so much.*
Or my strong father stalled by his hip after half
a block, leaning against a telephone pole.

ELEGY FOR THE GARDEN

What's she doing in the garden?
The boy wants his mother
to stop whatever it is and mind
him. It's the first warm day,
the very first, and she's hauling
a winter of rubbish. The fall was awful,
everything neglected, the winter
worse but now things want doing.
The green things want her. The garden steep,
in the mouth of the traffic;
everything growing there strong.
The boy gives up, heads over to a friend's.
She's too dirty to hug. One foot set on a rock,
the other on a bare bit of soil, she's more woman
than mother, more goat than woman.
She's almost parallel the incline,
tearing at what's dead, remembering
at last what she planted, what she loves.

Don't gawk,
the woman with the broom said.
Or didn't say, but I saw her face
as she went to her sweeping
as if that was the right thing to do.
It ate up the afternoon.
I've never seen blood like that —
a neat trail downhill, steady,
like it meant business.
The crunch I thought was metal on metal.
The woman with the broom
bringing a mug of water to the driver
who sat there drinking, shaking,
then set the mug on the curb.
The old guy curled around himself
on the pavement like that was his special place.
Sirens, cops, ambulance guys; they did CPR
and then they stopped. Even so
they were busy with it: yellow tape, cameras,
numbers called out across the hot concrete.
Finally they hosed down the pavement.
Someone must've been waiting,
fiddling with a purse or flicking channels.
I keep thinking of the shoe,
the one that landed on the woman's steps.
Stop sweeping, the cop said, *leave the shoe where it is.*

When it's bad, the plastic of the oxygen tent,
wavering intervention, comes between her and the room,
the square edges warble against her sight.
Back behind her head, to the left, where the corridor is,
the nursing station where help might come. In the daytime
carts roll down the corridor, chatter of china
on steel, silver covers on white plates of food
she can't eat. Where is the clock? Hitchcock clock
she can't see but feels, she can feel the hands move
and not move, move slow against the heaviness
of the room. She can't go into the corridor, she can
turn her head but she can't get up, she
can't get out of the bed, she wants her mother.
It's 3:15, 3:17, 3:21 she's waiting for four o'clock.
It's 4:02 her mother isn't here but suddenly
she stands at the foot of the bed it's alright
but the doctors say four to six. At six
her mother goes, takes her hands, takes her
voice away with her. The room goes grey
and the corridor that must be there is quiet
except for the nurses' voices.
Once, twice, they check in, good girl,
hand on her forehead. With the darkness
it comes down on her chest but if she's very still
it gets pushed to the edges. Breathe quiet now,
don't let it get you. Breathe quiet and believe
time is not still. Shadows slide along the bar of light
in the doorway. They're not alive. Something
makes those shadows the way something makes
the shadows that arc along the walls, the ceiling
of her room at home. Cars, their headlights.

The shadows go on and night doesn't end
and she learns you have to do what you can't do.
The nurses' voices begin to drift and she's
sliding down and then it's morning.

1.

I have no place to go but up, no way
to squeeze back down past faces and arms.
Goosebumps prickling my skin,
the elbows of older, taller children;
clammy grip of wet bathing suits.
My chin at someone's heels, someone else's chin
at my heels, we are a ladder of determination, up
and up to the five-metre platform.
My turn. Someone waits as I bring my arms back,
then swing them high, knees bent. Soft breath
behind me, as my toes tense at the edge,
knees, calves, thighs locked. Someone waits
but further down the line someone whispers,
jeers. I'm the girl who has decided to jump
but there's another I who will not proceed
and I stall in her body, its own decision,
until shame or stubbornness drives me forward at last
and down into a blue that receives but doesn't end me.

2.

A chute of intention has carried me here,
to the reconstructed cattle car
in Washington's Holocaust Museum.
Carried me through each tactful exhibit
so that I can see enough but not so much
that I stop seeing; has got me here
to the doorway but the dark interior, no.
No. In its wisdom, the body refuses
and I stall again until stubbornness or shame
drives me forward at last and it is as if
I were down into a dark that receives me,
my shoulder at someone's back, someone else's
shoulder at my back. Someone waits at my back, from
someone further down the line a crushed whisper.
We are a parcel of intention, but not our own.

JUNE ELEGY

Major Street, Toronto

The yard that has room in its heart for
one rosebush.
The yard with slim yellow irises.
The yard with gravel.
The yard with the wrought-iron fence,
box hedge; the gate snapping shut
like a change purse. The yard pursed.
The yard with roses that have no thorns, none,
the smell of raspberry jam.
The yard with columbine and columbine and columbine.
The yard with thistle & crab grass spiking two feet into the air.
The one wistful with wisteria, drooping.
The one with forget-me-nots in a filmy ring, trimmed lilac,
tea roses hand-cuffed to a stake, about to bloom.
The yard with garbage cans.
The yard with tricycles.
With sunlight.
Trash.
The yard with snow-in-summer, honey locust,
star-of-Bethlehem, periwinkle,
in bloom.

ELEGY FOR THE GIVEN

That on the southbound Bathurst bus
the voice at my elbow is speaking Russian,
the one at my back Portuguese perhaps, or Spanish.
That the air is grey and smells, as I walk down Bathurst,
successively, of exhaust, burnt toast, ozone,
alyssum. That on the north-east corner
of Bathurst and Bloor a man lies asleep or
unconscious or dead in his vomit and I walk by.
That on the south-east corner a middle-aged man
in shirtsleeves sells his god in a magazine
called *Awake* and all of us walk by.
That the young man going east on rollerblades
amid the cursing drivers has a ring through his eyebrow
and a peace symbol on his black leather jacket.
That at the Shoppers Drug Mart three blocks east
I can choose from 62 kinds of toothpaste.
That Rose of Sharon blooms
mauve to the south and white to the north
of the entry to the Aston Court. That
summer is come whether I want it or not.

ELEGY FOR THE GIFT (ELEGY FOR THE LIGHT)

Sometimes, when the subway car
comes briefly out of the tunnel,
we don't look up, miss the light.
And it's as though, inattentive,
we'd never had that moment
of brightness. A life might be full
of such small losses or full,
equally, of small, dense gifts:
the child on that same car
dipping her face into her mother's,
that perfect regard.

PARIS ELEGY (ATGET)

"How private and public spheres intersect" and
how it is observed, tacitly, that trees,
in twenty-five years, grow but buildings
do not; how light, how stillness, how
back lanes, courtyards, jumble and give
civil cohesion; how light bleeding in the gap
between buildings on the narrow street
dissolves the boundaries of walls, opens;
how people blur, are fugitive, illusive,
dark, concealed, afraid of what he will show
them, show of them; how the stones, edifices,
pavement emerge, in his lens, become beloved,
human.

What's the point, the sullen boy asks,
of learning their names? *Bird*
should do. The indistinct grey of wings
against concrete, droppings on the faded fence.
And in spring, a racket at dawn, nuisance
of yellow gum, smashed eggshell, white
or blue, on the hard-hearted pavement. And he's sullen
for a reason. The city hard this winter,
with its tests and arguments; its losses.
His mother in one house, father in another.
And now it's spring. So what. Birds,
and their names, and the guide
so sure it's important. Like an ache,
this arch of branch over his head, glint
of light on the water. Something moves
in the space between words. Streak of smeared white
on his left and a call. Gull.
He knows that one.
Dun, dumb gull, gullible;
gull diving for nothing, for his fake toss
off the ferry. The island phoney too,
little stretch of green at the city's edge,
its quiet, the lift of the leaves
against the wind. But the city's still there,
ten minutes across the harbour.
And this blue – but the water's trash too:
pop cans and plastic bags, gasoline slicks,
little spills like the eyes in peacock feathers.
Peacock names itself, but the others?
As if you could know them
by their names: house from song
sparrow, the black or the greyish streaks,
reddish tail or chestnut bar through the eyes.

Know them with your eyes closed:
three sweet notes, then a lower note, then
a trill; or chirp, cheep, and various twitters.
Song. House. Do they belong to him now, the way he
belongs to his mother, father, the way his parents belong
to him? As if words belonged to the things they name.
Things named for colour, the lilac lilac,
orange orange. What will the world give him
if he knows its names? House. Song. The word *snake*
leaping to his mouth at the striped ribbon at his feet,
its green slip through the grass.

Move: New Poems

SMALL CEREMONIES

Just us on the
cold blown rock. *Now,*
you say, lifting
the thick wool of
my sweater, the thin
wool below it, the grey
thermal cotton, the worn
cotton below, leaving
nothing between me and the world,
let's see what the wind has to say.

It didn't end the way we thought it would,
the road, the land it drove through which
wasn't Spain, wasn't Mexico, wasn't
anything we'd imagined. We'd coasted
the Pan-American for months, from village to city
to village, that big slide down mountains,
the butterflies I thought at first
were bluebirds, that big, but it wasn't
what we thought we were getting, and
the dust and the heat and all those little
borders and their little border guards,
fingers sly in our box of cookies.
We had dust and heat; rice and beans.
I thought we could fill up all
that emptiness with what we wanted it to be.
But we got tired, we got to what
we discovered was the end. Panama.
In that last town, in the ring, the dust,
the bull was in fact a cow and
with no ritual, no dignity, the matador
didn't kill anything. That afternoon we swam
in the shallows of the river, looking into the thin trees
that began the jungle, the Darien Gap, as if
we had a question it could answer,
a river full of villagers looking mildly at us.
We slept that night beside the river,
keeping company in that small faithful car.
It was time to go. In the darkness, I was
close to blind without my lenses, I was close
to blind, and when, in the night, something came
round the half-rolled windows, I could
see at first only shapes coming up around us
like our future, the one I thought

we could read. Shapes moving slowly,
curious, harmless, as they raised their
large mild heads to our windows
and wondered at us, a herd of cattle,
their white hides dark in the night,
shining in that night, harmless around us.
Me close to blind.

A SMALL THING

So here I am on a late summer evening,
late summer and the machinery of the body
is working smoothly, one foot in front of the other
and I'm only slightly drunk, only drunk enough
so that old, steady grief is dulled to a low hum.
I never thought I'd spend so much time
being the champion of loss. Never thought
I'd spend five years fighting it and five mourning.
It's not good to get struck down by distraction,
to get lost in the hum of your body, slightly drunk,
so that the young man on the bicycle unexpectedly
going down the sidewalk pings his bell at you,
and almost misses you. I mean almost doesn't miss.
I mean me, not you. I have a friend who bought her house
from a woman struck down, absurdly, by a bicycle,
struck down and not killed but not alive either,
the machinery of her body a low hum now among
the hum of machines. It seems like such a small thing.
What does it feel like living in the house
of a woman who isn't alive and isn't dead.

SCARE

January 29, 2002

She had ten years on me,
the doctor. She wasn't looking
at me, she was watching the screen,
one hand expertly stroking
the dumb snout of the ultrasound
over and then over and again over
my right breast,
her fine face focussed.

She wasn't looking at me
but all I wanted to look at
was her human face.

For months I forget.
She wastes and wastes, my aunt.
The nurses tend her absent body
and she grows into nothing.
Even her sons, who loved,
love her, almost stop visiting.
Nobody home.

My own parents complete,
alive, I wake in the night,
gasping, from a dream of the old house –
a bear, compost brown, shuffling
in the basement. A presence
we quietly live with,
afraid.

She used to make us laugh.

TAKING IT IN

I call to ask you about property taxes
and you tell me about the light.
Every time I call, my prudent
father, you tell me about the light,
the way it comes in through the window
and moves over the floor, over
the kitchen table, how it lays hands
on everything. And I listen, and see
you at the kitchen table in Winnipeg,
the crisp blue sky a rectangle
in the window. Oh love.
That gives me a window
like this, a father, light.
I think you are going
like oak, like brandy, like
dark wine. The good stuff
you're made of taking the light in.

A mumbled chant, the words run
through my head as I soap each finger,
thumb; the back of each hand and
up the wrists: *Happy birthday to you,*
not looking in the mirror. *Happy birthday,*
happy birthday, closing the tap with a paper towel,
elbowing open the door to the Women's,
happy birthday to you, not wanting to touch
what others have touched, has touched them.
Even before SARS, that April people
drowned in their lungs. Back when my son
was little and in and out of hospital, the nurse
in Emerg took my wrist in the waiting room,
whispered, "They process the meningitis cases here;
be careful of your kid," and showed me the tap trick.
I didn't want my son to suffer what other children suffered,
be touched by what had touched them. The singing,
though, didn't start till that SARS spring when it was
happening here. I didn't want to be touched,
to suffer what other people suffered; wanted
to be missed in that swathe. My friend who works
at Mount Sinai gave me "Happy Birthday"
to count the twenty seconds you need for clean.
The words run through, I sing myself safe;
who knows what they carry with them?
Sing myself past the birthday girl or boy, though
sometimes I must say *to me,* wishing
myself another year, wishing myself someplace
away from contagion, from the suffering of others,
what they carry with them; away from cancer,
which isn't a germ, from terrorist bombs
opening commuter trains, though they're not

germs either. Wishful thinking, that chant,
though there is a reason for all this;
there's a reason we're not safe.
Feed lots and frankenfoods; chickens with their
beaks cut off. And capital. And callousness.
It's what we've done. It's what
we've done, not what we haven't done,
that's put us here. While everything we love shifts
under the weight of everything we do to it.

A Day

This is the day I find everything lost:
car keys burrowed into the ooze of leaves
in the rain, beside the garbage can;
the mate to the earring my sister gave me
that year I finally pierced my ears; the watch
tossed sleepily into a Kleenex box
in the dark at midnight after I switched off the TV.
What more might I find on a day like this? The sun
rising at Eilat, the dark herd of goats
that browsed through our campsite,
the Bedouin we spoke to with our hands,
you with your camera at dawn, your eye
for the spectacular, for nooks of beauty,
your great gusts of joy, you?

MOVE

It's been fifteen, no, sixteen
years and for the first time
you think about moving,
about what you could take with you,
what you'd leave behind.
And then you imagine that everything
you've borrowed, everything
you've lent, everything taken or sold
will be returned, things will come into
and leave the house that soon will be
not your house anymore, it will empty
and fill and come to rest
and everything will begin and
everything will end.

AUTHOR'S NOTES:

Thanks to Erin Mouré's "Ocean Poem" (*Furious*, House of Anansi, 1988) for the locution of the second line in "Elegy for Knowing" (3).

The epigram in Spanish in "List (Elegy)" is from Pablo Neruda's poem, *"La Canción Desesperada"* [The Song of Despair] in *Veinte Poemas de Amor y Una Canción Desesperada* [Twenty Love Poems and a Song of Despair]. Translation the author's.

The phrase in quotations in "Paris Elegy (Atget)" is from the catalogue for the exhibit "Paris Itineraries: Photographs by Eugène Atget", shown at the Art Gallery of Ontario in March, 2001.